Save Energy

Kay Barnham

WAYLAND

Copyright © Wayland 2006
Editor: Penny Worms
Senior Design Manager: Rosamund Saunders
Designer: Ben Ruocco, Tall Tree Ltd

Published in Great Britain in 2006 by Wayland,
an imprint of Hachette Children's Books

British Library Cataloguing in Publication Data
Barnham, Kay
    Saving energy. - (Environment action)
    1. Energy conservation - Juvenile literature
    I. Title
    333.7'916

ISBN 10: 0 7502 4868 8
ISBN 13: 978 0 7502 4868 6

Printed in China
Wayland
An imprint of Hachette Children's Books
338 Euston Road, London NW1 3BH

The publishers would like to thank the following for allowing us to
reproduce their pictures in this book:
Alamy: 25 (Maggie Murray). Corbis images: 15 (Svenja-Foto). Ecoscene:
title page and 12 (Genevieve Leaper), 5 (Peter Currell), 8 (Jon Bower), 9
(Michael Gore), 11 (Michael Cuthbert), 13 (Paul Thompson), 17 (Paul
Kennedy), 20 (Vicki Coombs), 24 (Peter Cairns), 29 (Bruce Harber).
Getty images: cover and 27 (Mike Brinson), 4 (Angelo Cavalli), 7 (Bruce
Forster), 10 (Peter Sterling), 16 (Larry Dale Gordon), 18 (David
Noton), 22 (Kevin Cooley), 23 (Donna Day), 26 (Vivid Images), 28 (Paul
Harris). NASA Images: 14. Wayland Picture Library: 6, 21. With special
thanks to the Marketing team at Honda (UK) and Honda Dream Factory
for the Honda Civic Hybrid image on page 19.

Contents

What is Energy? 4

Why Save Energy? 6

Climate Change 8

A Cleaner World 10

Wind Energy 12

Solar Energy 14

Water Energy 16

Transport 18

Use it Again! 20

Switch it Off! 22

Saving Energy at Home 24

Saving Energy at School 26

More Ideas! 28

Glossary 30

Index 32

What is Energy?

Energy makes things work. We use energy in an unbelievable number of ways. It is used to make aeroplanes fly. It is used to make lifts go up and down. Energy is used to heat our homes.

△ Without energy, these funfair rides would be dark, silent and still.

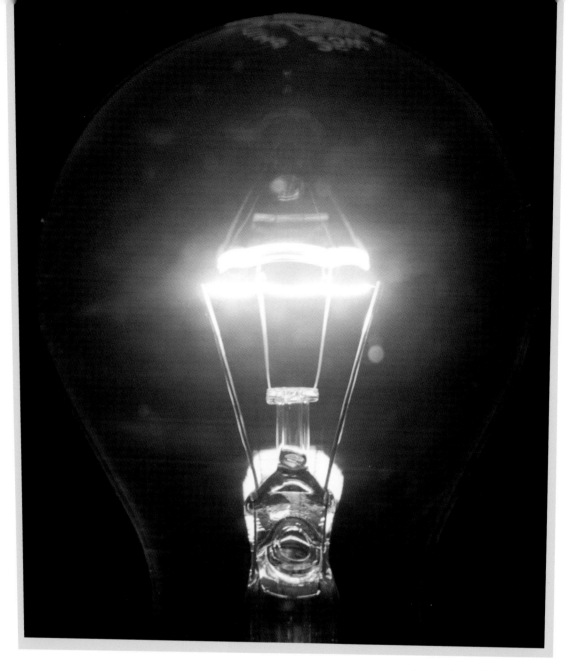

Coal, oil and gas give us energy. Coal is burnt in power stations to generate **electricity**, which gives us light and heat. It also makes machines work. Oil can be used to make fuel for our cars. We use gas to cook with and to heat our homes. Wind, sunlight and water can also give us energy.

△ It takes electricity to make a light bulb glow.

Why Save Energy?

Oil, coal and gas are known as **fossil fuels**. They were formed millions of years ago, long before the dinosaurs. Every day, more fossil fuels are being taken from the ground. But there isn't an endless supply. Once they are gone, they are gone for ever.

△ An oil rig is a platform that stands in the middle of the sea. It pumps oil from beneath the seabed.

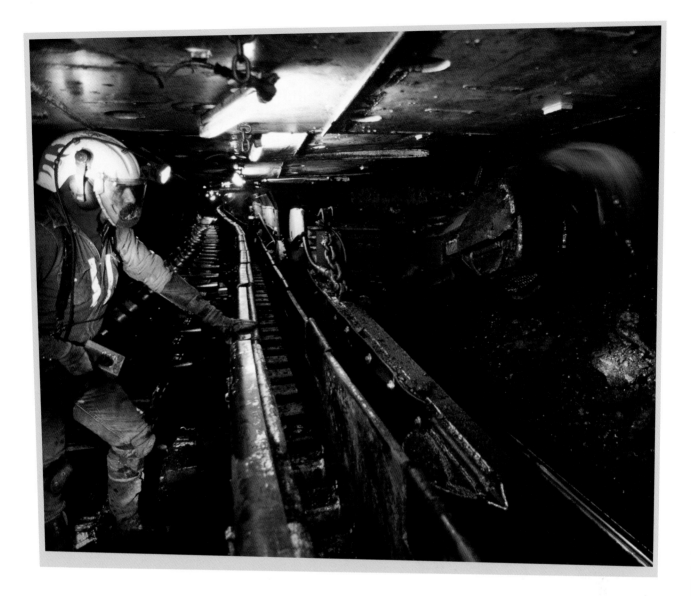

Right now, we have enough fossil fuels to provide energy for everyone. But if we keep using as much energy as we do, these supplies will run out. By using less energy, our oil, coal and gas will last longer.

△ Coal is dug from mines, deep below the earth's surface.

Climate Change

Our planet is getting warmer. Many experts believe that our activities are causing this climate change. Power stations, factories, homes, aeroplanes and cars all send **carbon dioxide** into the air. This gas stays in the earth's **atmosphere**, trapping the sun's heat.

△ When coal is burnt in old-style power stations, it produces a huge amount of carbon dioxide.

△ As the earth becomes warmer, polar ice melts. Polar bears have fewer places to hunt and less to eat.

Climate change will create problems for wildlife and coastal areas. Higher temperatures will melt the ice in the **Arctic** and **Antarctic** and cause sea levels to rise. They might also cause the weather to change.

FACT!

Closing down just one coal-fired power station would stop another two million tonnes of carbon dioxide entering our atmosphere.

A Cleaner World

Wind, sun and water energy do not produce carbon dioxide when they are turned into electricity. Best of all, they are types of **renewable energy**, which means they are never going to run out. By using renewable energy, we will use less fossil fuels. Oil, coal and gas supplies will last longer and our world will be a less **polluted** place.

▽ The wind's energy is powerful. See how it drives this windsurfer through the water.

Transporting oil to where it is needed can also cause pollution. It is shipped by sea in huge **tankers**, carrying millions of litres of oil. Tankers can be damaged during bad weather, losing their loads and polluting the sea and coasts for miles around.

△ Oil spills cause great harm to sea birds. Coated with oil, they may be unable to fly. They could poison themselves when trying to clean their feathers.

Wind Energy

A wind **turbine** is a machine that turns the wind's energy into electricity. As the wind blows, the blades turn. The stronger the wind, the more electricity there will be. One wind turbine can provide enough energy for 600 homes.

The blades on a wind turbine are shaped like aeroplane wings to catch the passing wind.

Wind turbines are built in windy places. A group of wind turbines is called a wind farm, and some are built at sea where the wind is strongest.

◁ Wind energy is not a new idea. Windmills work in nearly the same way. But, instead of producing electricity, they are used to **grind** grain into flour.

13

Solar Energy

The sun gives us light and heat. But its rays can also be turned into energy for us to use. This is called **solar energy**.

△ The International **Space Station** has huge solar panels to capture the sun's energy and power the Station when it is in space.

Solar panels are used to collect solar energy. The panels are put in places that get the most sunlight, like roofs. When the sun shines, the panels warm up and this warmth can be turned into electricity or used to heat water.

△ Solar panels are best suited to countries with hot, sunny weather.

Water Energy

Tides, **dams**, **waterfalls** and waves can all be used to produce electricity. As fast-flowing water gushes towards a waterfall or through a dam, it turns huge turbines. These generate electricity for us to use.

△ A dam is a large wall built across a river valley to hold back water. This is the Hoover Dam in the USA which provides enough electricity for 1.3 million people.

△ New **technology** is also being developed to turn wave energy into electricity.

Tidal barrages are barriers built where the sea meets a large river. As the tides flow in and out, the water turns turbines which produce electricity.

Transport

Travelling in cars, aeroplanes, and even buses and trains uses precious fossil fuels. It also creates even more pollution than homes or factories. If more people travelled together, it would save energy and create less pollution.

▷ Buses and trains carry lots of passengers. They use much less fuel than if all the people made their journey separately by car.

Engineers are developing new aeroplanes that use less energy. Cars are already on sale that use two types of energy – petrol and electricity. These **hybrid** cars use petrol at high speeds, but make and store electricity as they travel. The electricity is then used at low speeds.

△ Hybrid cars use less petrol than normal cars. They are better for the environment too.

Use it Again!

It can take a large amount of energy to make brand-new things. For example, new paper is made from wood. Trees need to be felled and chopped into pieces before they are taken to the paper mill. Recycled paper is simply made from old paper. By re-using or recycling things, we can save lots of energy.

◁ Recycled glass is made by melting old glass in a **furnace**. The temperature can be much lower than when making new glass. This saves energy.

You can recycle paper, cardboard, cans, glass bottles and jars, batteries and plastic bottles. As well as saving energy, recycling reduces the amount of rubbish that is thrown away too.

 Many homes now collect items for recycling. Most towns and cities have recycling facilities.

Switch it Off!

When televisions, computers and lamps are switched on, they use electricity. When they are switched off, they don't. So, by switching things off when you're not using them, you'll save energy. Your parents will be pleased too – they'll have a smaller electricity bill!

Having all the lights on in your house uses lots of energy. If you leave a room, turn the light off!

▷ To save energy, don't switch off your television using the remote control. Push the button on the television instead.

If you can see any lights on the front of a television, DVD player or washing machine, it isn't really 'off'. It is only on 'stand-by'. This still uses energy.

FACT!

In the UK, it takes the energy of two power stations to power all the televisions that are left on stand-by.

Saving Energy at Home

There are many ways you can help to save energy at home. For example, when you leave the house, turn the heating thermostat down or switch the heating off. This will save heating fuel.

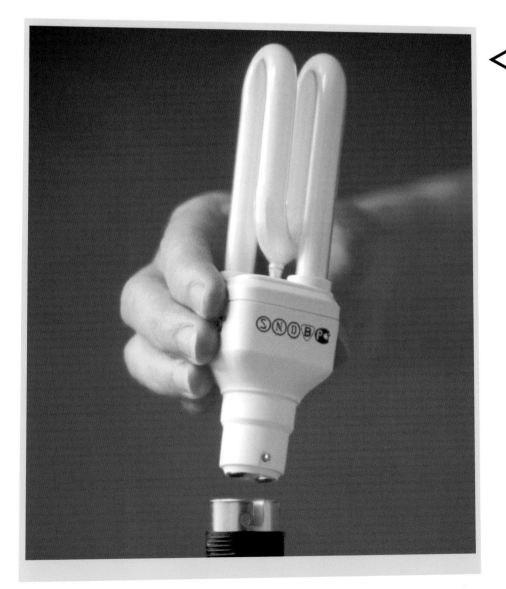

◁ Low-energy light bulbs are just as bright as normal bulbs. They are more expensive to buy, but they save energy and last much longer.

If you only run washing machines and dishwashers when they are full, you will save energy.

Draughty doors and windows make houses colder. A **draught excluder** is a good way of solving this problem. Your house will stay warmer and you'll use less energy. Also, encourage your parents to boil only as much water as they need for their hot drinks. The kettle will boil faster and save energy.

FACT!

Did you know that it takes less energy to keep a freezer cold when it is full? If there are any gaps, you can fill these with scrunched-up paper.

25

Saving Energy at School

How good is your school at saving energy? If windows and doors are left open during the winter, heat will escape. Keeping them shut saves energy. Also, classrooms have lots of lights which use up lots of energy! The last person to leave a room should turn them off.

Turn the computer off when you have finished using it. Leaving it on stand-by will waste energy.

△ If you cycle to school, you won't get stuck in a traffic jam!

Many children use up a great deal of energy going to and from school – they travel by car. Travelling with friends is a good way to save energy. Even better, why not walk or cycle? It's healthy exercise and you'll use no petrol at all!

More Ideas!

Would you believe that buying food at farmers' markets is a good way to save energy? Often, the vegetables you see in supermarkets will have been flown or driven thousands of kilometres to reach the shelves. Food grown at a local farm will have travelled only a few kilometres, using much less fuel.

△ Supermarkets need energy for lighting and heating, and to run the freezers and tills. Markets use very little energy.

Insulation in houses is thick padding in lofts and inside walls. It stops heat escaping from the house and so less energy is needed to keep the house warm. But did you know that some people plant grass on their roofs, to keep in the heat?

These houses in Denmark were built to use as little energy as possible.

Glossary

Antarctic – the land and sea surrounding the South Pole

Arctic – the land and sea surrounding the North Pole

Atmosphere – the air around the earth

Carbon dioxide – a type of gas in the air

Dams – strong walls built across river valleys to hold back water

Draught excluder – something that stops cold air getting through gaps in windows and doors

Draughty – when cold air blows into a house or room

Electricity – the power or energy used to give light and heat and to work machines

Engineers – people who make machines or plan the building of roads and bridges

Fossil fuels – natural fuels, such as coal, oil or gas that formed long ago

Furnace – a very hot oven, where things are melted

Grind – to crush into small pieces

Hybrid – something that is made by putting two different things together

Mines – man-made holes under the ground where things are taken from the earth

Polluted – when air or water become dirty or unhealthy

Recycling facilities – a place where you can recycle things

Renewable energy – energy that does not disappear once it has been used

Solar energy – energy that comes from the sun

Solar panels – special panels that capture the sun's rays to turn it into electricity or heat water

Space station – a large building in space that travels round the earth, where astronauts can stay

Tankers – very large ships that carry oil

Technology – using knowledge to make or do things

Tidal barrages – barriers built where the sea meets a large river to generate electricity

Tides – the daily rise and fall of the level of the sea

Turbine – a spinning rotor that turns when air or water rushes through it to generate electricity

Valley – a deep dip in the land, usually containing a flowing river

Waterfalls – rivers of water falling from a high place to a low place

Index

carbon dioxide   8–9, 10
cars and transport   4–5, 18–19, 27, 28
climate change   8–9
coal   5, 6–7, 8–9, 10
dam   16
electricity   5, 10, 12–13, 15, 16–17, 19, 22–27
fossil fuels   6–7, 10, 18
fuel   5, 18–19, 27, 28
gas   5, 6–7, 8, 10
heating   4–5, 15, 25, 26, 28–29
houses   18, 22, 25, 29
lighting   4–5, 22–23, 24, 26, 28
oil   5, 6–7, 10–11
oil spills   11
pollution   10–11, 18
power stations   5, 8–9, 23
recycling   20–21
renewable energy   10, 12–17
saving electricity
        at home   22–25, 28–29
        at school   26–27
solar energy   5, 10, 14–15
solar panels   14–15
sun   5, 8, 10, 14–15
turbines   12, 13, 16–17
water energy   5, 10, 16–17
wave energy   17
weather   9, 11
wildlife   9, 11
wind energy   5, 10, 12–13